# LET ME SHOW

# YOU HOW I

# LOVE YOU

## BY JIM CULLUM

### ILLUSTRATION: JACOB HUGHES

No part of this publication may be reproduced, stored in a retrieval system or transmitted in any form or by any means, electronic, mechanical, photographic including photocopying, recording or otherwise without prior written permission of the publisher.

ISBN-13: 978-1502548566

ISBN-10:1502548569

# Dedication

This book is dedicated to all the people who want to be in love, who are already in love and wish to express it more passionately, and to those who will someday find love when the time is right and enjoy honoring that love every day.

I dedicate this book as well to all the parents (especially the dads) who want their daughters to find partners who will show their love for them rather than lust for them and for all the moms who want their sons to treat their loves with respect and kindness and show it each day.

I am also dedicating this book to my dad who died when I was 12 years old. He was a kind, generous and loving man. I am sure he did not coin this phrase but he always said it, "It's nice to be important, but it's more important to be nice."

# Acknowledgements

My sincerest appreciation goes to Mary Cullum, my special love, who has allowed me to test on her all the wonderful ideas that are in this book. It's been fun and exciting coming up with the many creative ways to express my love and positive feelings.

I wish express my gratitude to everyone who has helped me along the way; from my dad who taught me many lessons early on in life, to the good friends who have encouraged me to put all my thoughts on paper.

Special thanks to Kanta Bosniak who has worked with me during countless hypnosis and coaching sessions to enhance my creativity and pull it all together. Your tireless energy, guidance and work putting the physical book in shape is greatly appreciated.

Thanks to Dr. Walter E. Brackelmanns, who has been a colleague and friend for almost 25 years. Your insights and remarkable stories about couple's therapy taught me that there are no limits to the wonderful possibilities.

Special thanks to Christie Liberio for her creative design ideas and all the work she has done on the computer. Sincere thanks to Jacob Hughes for his creativity and design ideas. Many thanks to all the friends and family members who are too numerous to mention, but have commented on the different ways I have expressed my love and feelings, letting me know that, "I did a good job" doing many of the things that I have done over the years.

# TABLE OF CONTENTS

# SECTION ONE

# SECTION TWO

# FUN THINGS THAT COUPLES

# CAN DO TOGETHER

SLOWER TRAVEL –

# Foreword

By: Walter E. Brackelmanns, M.D.

I have known Jim Cullum as a friend and colleague for 25 years. As you will see when you read this book, Jim is smart, kind, considerate, sensitive, knowledgeable and intuitive. This is a book written primarily for men, to be purchased and read by women, who will then make notes about what they want and like, and then give the book to their man for his education and consideration. Jim's intuitiveness and sensitivity toward his wife and women in general is remarkable. I believe this is a very important book that has been long in coming. As a psychiatrist who has specialized exclusively in treating couples for 40 years, I can certainly attest to the fact that Jim Cullum has identified and illustrated virtually all the key components to creating and maintaining a growing, loving and fulfilling relationship and marriage. One of the things that makes Jim's book intriguing is that he has successfully captured the difference between men and women, and the essence of what women really need in relationships.

To the men reading this book: Have you found the romance and intimacy, that spark that use to be in your relationship, missing? Do you feel that every day is the same old same old? A woman is moved to wanting to be affectionate, loving and sexual not by what she feels in her body but by how she is treated. This is the work of Rosemary Basson, Clinical Professor at the University of British Columbia, Vancouver, Canada and Beverly Whipple, Professor Emeritus at Rutgers University in New Brunswick, New Jersey. Imagine a large circle with the woman in the middle of the circle. On the circle are all the things that a woman wants and likes. She may like holding, cuddling, kissing, touching, holding hands and an endless number of others things that may be sexual, or just sensitive and responsive to her and her needs. The key words here are *want and like.* This will show her that you are sensitive to her needs, you care about her, and you are responsive to what will please her.

If you look at the table of contents, you will see a wide variety of items that your wife or honey might want from you. The items that she wants and likes would go on her circle such as a simple back rub, sending cards or flowers, taking her out to dinner or any of the other wonderful suggestions that Jim offers in this complete book about how to please your mate. She might ask for one of those items or you might surprise her with what you believe (and perhaps even know) would please her.

As I read this book, and I did read it very carefully, I was impressed with several things. The most important item is paying attention to your wife, life-mate or girlfriend, which Jim talks about over and over. Be sensitive to her needs and feelings. Jim suggests you listen and learn about who she is and what she wants. File that information away for future reference, like a special occasion. By the way, a special occasion can be any time you think about your honey.

That last point I want to make is something that Jim subtly and not so subtly addresses throughout this book. The message is listen, pay attention and be responsive. Jim emphasizes these points in Section One under communication, learn to listen, pay attention and ask lots of questions. I want to underline the importance of listening and add talking to it. There are six methods of communication. These are *play-talk or bantering, information exchange, casual conversation, intellectual discussion, talking and listening and the Dialogue of Intimacy*. Intimacy is a conscious process of trying to understand who another person is separate from self and transmitting who you are as a separate autonomous person and vice versa.

The instruments used in the Dialogue of Intimacy are *talking and listening.* Talking means talking about negative or positive feelings in the context of self, with no expectation from the other person other than she will try to understand. Listening is the counterpart to that. Listening is hearing what the other person says in the context of that person with no reference back to self, without taking anything personally. Taking it personally means that you interpret what the other person is saying based on your inner world rather than her inner world. It is the negative feelings that give us trouble. I am making a distinction between emotions and feelings.

Emotions are things like fear, anger, joy, sadness, frustration, happiness, anxiety, depression and more. Feelings are the negative beliefs that you have about yourself. These are feelings of inadequacy, worthlessness, incompetence, being a failure, being weak, being unattractive, being sexual inept, and more. These feelings we have about ourselves are feelings, but are never facts. These feelings may match reality, but they are never facts. It is important to listen and understand, but do not try to fix the inner world of the other person. You will fail. Ask the other person what you can do to be helpful. Do not be responsible for the other person's inner world, but do be responsive.

A very important thing to consider when you are in the world of feelings or doing the Dialogue of Intimacy is that *in that world there is no right or wrong, there is no good or bad, there is no agenda and there is no reality.* By this I mean that perception rules. You do not argue to get the facts straight. That will shut off communication faster than anything except *criticizing and defending.* We call this the *Dialogue of Distance.* When doing the Dialogue of Intimacy there are four taboos. *There should be no criticizing, no defending, no demanding and no uncontrolled or vented anger.* Uncontrolled anger means I am so angry I can't listen. Vented anger is anger openly vented toward another person.

It is this Dialogue of Intimacy that connects us to our mate. Listening and trying to understand is the highest form of caring. If you understand what is bothering your honey and you love her, you will want to be responsive. Being responsive can sometimes feel like you are giving up a portion of yourself, and that can sometimes feel like you are giving up the totality of yourself. What I am saying is the Dialogue of Intimacy is not easy, but it is the best gift that one lover, mate or friend can give to another.

My recommendation is that you read this book carefully and follow the suggestions. The payoff will be enormous. I also recommend that that you and your honey set aside 15 minutes or less on two different days and practice talking and listening. This is being with each other in the present. We call this quality time and mindfulness. Eleanor Roosevelt said, "Yesterday is history, tomorrow is a mystery and today is a gift. That's why we call it the present." We only have the present. That is why it is so important to do wonderful things for each other and with each other. For more information on the Dialogue of Intimacy you can go to CouplesLifeLine.com, askdrb.com, or aacast.net.

Do what Jim Cullum says, and you will have a growing evolving marriage and/or relationship, instead of a static one.

Walter E. Brackelmanns, M.D.

By:  Rev. Kanta Bosniak

I have known Jim Cullum for over fifteen years as a colleague, leader in the field of human potential development and friend. I first met him at a conference at which we were both presenters and I liked him right away. I was impressed with his communication skills, wisdom, depth, humor, and likeability. Not only is he a great speaker, but he really listens and he knows how to make real connections with people.

These same interpersonal abilities work in his personal life. Jim is one half of a very happy and lasting marriage. Throughout dating, courtship, marriage, parenthood and grandparenthood, Jim has prioritized his relationship with his wife and sweetheart, Mary. He once described himself to me as a "true romantic," which in his case does not mean that he is not realistic, far from it. He realistically knows that to build something good, you have to really want it and you have to invest the time, care and energy to make it work and keep it working.

Jim knows how to build relationships and like any good teacher or coach, he knows how to share his knowledge. In this book, he does just that. Readers will learn practical information about how to show their girlfriends, fiancées and wives how they are loved and how to keep the romantic relationship going strong.

We often hear discussions, usually comedic, about what women want. Supposedly, this is a deep and unfathomable mystery. As a woman, I can tell you it's actually pretty simple. Women (healthy ones, anyway) want to be cherished. They want to know their significant other wants them specifically and is paying attention to who they are. They want to be valued. They want to feel embraced by and enfolded in the love of their sweetheart. And above all, they want to be shown this love not only in the first stages of dating, but in day-to-day life as their relationship develops and matures.

When I interview couples prior to writing their wedding ceremony and I hear their love stories, the importance of meeting these needs shows up. When a man loves a woman and is willing to show her that love, relationship magic happens. When couples tell me about the fun things they do together, their eyes light up. I see them positively basking in one another's presence.

In this book, readers will gain insight and practical techniques in both of these important components of a successful relationship. In the first section, you will discover great ways to show your sweetie how you love her. In the second, you'll enjoy a smorgasbord of fun things you can do together. In addition, Jim has included many links for further exploration and discovery.

I think this book is excellent, a helpful resource and one that is important culturally. When men connect with their girlfriends and wives and build happier relationships, they model healthier and happier relational habits for others, especially their children. And everyone benefits!

Rev. Kanta Bosniak, author of **Abundance Triggers**, **Awakened Love**, and **Twin Flames**

# Introduction

One day while thinking about the things in my life that I do pretty well, I realized I am a good "people person" and I decided to write this book. Over the years, I have been complimented by several friends about the way I do things for my wife as well as other people I care about. I enjoy seeing her smile and laugh and seeing the way she gets that warm look in her eyes when I do something with a little extra effort. It really takes no special talent to show the one you love how much love you have to share. Everything I do can be easily learned and duplicated; you just have to want to be nice. Desire is the key to making someone else happy. When you truly desire to show someone how you feel, they feel it too.

There are many ways to show the one you love how much you really care. Anyone can say, "I love you." Remember that actions speak louder than words. Doing those small (and sometimes large) things that **show** how you feel about someone leaves very powerful impressions. Let's explore different ways that can be fun and very meaningful to your lover (and to you). It does not matter if you are single and dating, living together, or married for many years, you can always learn something new to show your significant other how special they are and how you feel about them.

There are over 100 links in this book that have been listed to allow you to explore in greater detail, the different areas I present to you. These links are all accurate and working as of October, 2014. Please consult your local phone directory or internet WEB browser for further information.

# A WONDERFUL EXAMPLE

# TO SHARE WITH YOU

I'd like to start by giving you one example of how I set up the second Valentine's Day that I shared with my wife. It was a combination of several ideas that I put together, similar to how an artist creates a collage. My wife had a day job and was out of the house to 5:00 PM. I started making notes several days in advance to make sure everything would happen exactly as I had imagined it.

When she arrived home from work (Valentine's Day) she noticed the vase with a dozen long-stem red roses on the table and thanked me for them. I told her that I wanted to give her a nice hot-oil massage. We went to the bedroom where I had a large bath towel spread out on her side of the bed. I had a bottle of scented massage oil in the bathroom sink soaking in warm water to warm the oil. As she was lying on her belly, I started at her neck and slowly massaged the oil all the way down to her toes. It took about 25 to 30 minutes to do this. By the way, she loves to get massages.

After the massage, I wanted her to take a nice warm bath as I prepared dinner for us. When she entered the bathroom, the next phase was already in motion. I had prepared the tub (as I was giving her the massage) with warm water and her favorite bath oil. The lights were all turned off and I had several scented candles lit and placed around the bathroom. They were on the tub, on the sink, on the toilet tank and even a couple of candles on the floor near the tub. (Note - some were unscented and the rest were all in her favorite scent. Too many scents might be overpowering).

I actually bought eighteen red roses and after arranging twelve in the vase on the table, I set six aside. I pulled the petals off the six roses I had set aside just before she came home and right after the massage, I sprinkled them around the bathroom. They were on the sink, on the tub, in the tub, on the floor and all over. I had the tape player on the vanity playing Italian Love Songs that she likes. I told her to relax in the tub and I'd call her when dinner was ready.

Next phase took place in the kitchen. I had bought a bottle of wine; a blush that I know she likes. I had shrimp cocktail, two lobster tails and a nice steak on the menu. We had string beans, baked potatoes and mushrooms sautéed in wine and butter. Two dinner candles were lit and I turned off the lights. After I had cooked the dinner, we enjoyed a great meal with the tape still playing the love songs in the background.

After dinner we began the next phase, a retreat into the living room for some after-dinner drinks and little pastries.  As she poured the drinks I cleared the table. It makes life easier having a dishwasher but this is not necessary. By the way, drinks can be any of any variety: coffee, tea, sparkling cider or juice. They do not have to be alcoholic. The night was wonderful and so romantic. That was one way to spend a warm and loving Valentine's Day at home.

The first Valentine's Day we shared was very special! I bought her flowers and a box of candy. She was very happy and really appreciated it. This second time I wanted to outdo myself. I wanted to be different and not do the "same old same old." When you really care about someone, it's important to show them that you do care and are not just saying it. Talk is cheap!

A note: I mention several WEB sites throughout this book as a source of information for the reader. I have no affiliation with these sites although I may have personally used some of them for my own benefit. They are all accurate at the time of publication.  If you are unable to locate a site or desire further information, please use your search engine or phone directory to locate sources for yourself.

Please be aware! You can bend over backwards for someone to show them how much you really love them, but that never guarantees that they will love you back. Money is no issue here. Multi-millionaires have given away vast amounts of their money to entice someone to "love them," only to feel the pain of rejection anyway. If someone does not want to love you for who you are, you are much better off without them. People come in a vast variety of sizes, shapes and colors; there is someone for everyone. We become so hung-up on who we don't have in our lives we fail to simply turn around to see who is standing right there waiting for us. Doing everything in this book will not guarantee that your lover will love you more, but it will certainly show them and everyone else how attentive and caring you are.

Awareness number two! If someone treats you less than wonderfully, you do not need them in your life. Life is too short to hang on to uncaring people. A great partner is one who truly cares about you and enjoys showing it. Lying is a no-no. A rule of thumb I have is, if a person will lie about anything they will lie about everything. A real relationship is based on mutual trust. That trust grows stronger each day. One lie can destroy it all in an instant.

# MUTUAL RESPECT

It's absolutely necessary for both parties in a relationship to have respect for each other. This should be non-negotiable. You cannot really love someone if you do not have respect for them, and they cannot really love you if they have no respect for you. If you find yourself in a relationship and you realize your partner has little or no respect for you or your feelings, removing yourself from that relationship is the best possible solution for you. No matter what one tries to say to you, it's their actions that truly express their feelings.

It's interesting although sad that some people will resort to any means to attract someone. They will tell a potential partner ANYTHING they think they want to hear to create a relationship. Remember that actions speak louder than words.

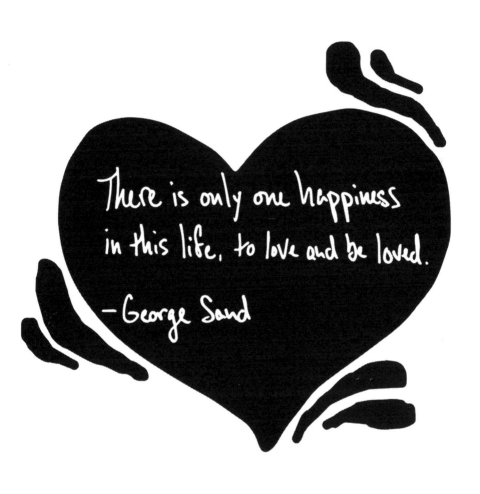

There is only one happiness in this life, to love and be loved.

—George Sand

Use this space for notes, thoughts and your own
ideas:

# COMMUNICATION

Communication is the way we share information with each other. We communicate in a wide variety of ways. The easiest form of communication is talking with someone. Two or more people have a conversation and share their thoughts, ideas, feelings and more. Please know that words are just one small part of the communication process. When you are talking with your honey, look into her eyes as you speak. They say the eyes are the window into the soul. Look at her face and notice the shape and structure of her face as she talks. You'll notice that when people are talking, their eyes or their face does not always seem to agree with what they are saying with their mouth. We sometimes say what we think the other person wants to hear but we may not actually agree with what we are saying. A person's eyes or face should look relaxed and comfortable with the words coming from their mouth. It's best to say what you mean and mean what you say. Honesty is quite important.

I'd like to mention a word on texting. It seems that everyone today is texting. I personally find texting impersonal and cold. Yes, at times it is necessary but when one partner texts the other partner to come down for dinner; that to me is simply cold. Sure, you can add little graphics and symbols (smiley faces, winks, etc.) to add emphasis to your texts but I prefer communication between two people to be a face-to-face interaction. I want to hear the tone of your voice, look into your eyes, see the way you might turn your head or even your nose! I do not want to "guess" what you are really saying behind the phone.

# LEARN TO LISTEN

Listening is a skill and anyone can learn to do it. We all hear the things that our lover says but do we listen to what they are saying? Learn to pay attention to the conversation and you'll be amazed at what you can discover from what is being said. It has been said that we have two ears and one mouth so we should be listening twice as much as speaking. I've created many wonderful surprises for my "other half" simply by listening to what was being said and later acting on it. The events I am relating to in this book were all things that I have done to express my feelings to my lover simply because I knew (from listening) that she would appreciate them.

You might overhear your honey talking to her best friend about a perfume she really likes or the color of a blouse she wants to get. Make mental notes or write them down if you have to. I remember hearing my wife (girlfriend at the time) talking about a vocal group she liked and I bought her the album a few weeks later as a birthday gift. That would be a CD or MP3 now but it's the point that counts. It's those casual things that one says during a conversation that can later become a real asset when you act upon them.

# PAY ATTENTION

(Using your senses: sight, smell, hearing, etc.)

Learn to become aware of your lover and how she presents herself. Notice her hair; new style, new color, new smell (shampoos and body wash will leave a scent).  Let your lover know that you have noticed that she took the time to make a nice change. This shows her that you are attentive and that you appreciate the effort she took to do what she did.

Is she wearing a new style of clothing or maybe the jewelry you bought for her? Small comments like, "That necklace (bracelet, earrings, or whatever it is) looks very nice on you," means a lot. Is she wearing a different perfume?  By paying attention to what she likes, you will begin to learn to "shop" for your lover as mentioned later on in this book. When you really care about someone, you pay attention to them and notice (again with all your senses) the things they like as well as the things they do not like.

In the event that your honey has made a change that you do not care for, remember to be tactful. Yes, it's always best to be honest but you can "be honest" in a productive way.  Rather than say,

"That blouse looks horrible on you, you might say it like this, "The blouse you are wearing doesn't quite flatter your eyes (or face or hair) and you know how much I love the way your eyes (or face or hair) look." It's best to pay an honest compliment along with a negative remark. It's just being tactful rather than hurtful. No one cares to have their feelings hurt.

# ASK LOTS OF QUESTIONS

Please understand that the human being was designed with four openings in the head to receive information and only one opening in the head from which to give it. If you talk more than you listen, you'll never learn anything about your honey. This goes for new friendships, as well as couples married more than 25 years! My wife never liked the water and she never learned how to swim, however we were married over twenty years when she first told me she wanted to try riding on a wave runner!

Ask questions and listen to the answers too! Find out likes and dislikes so you know what to look for and what to avoid. Even though I am a certified scuba diver, I never pushed for any water activities as a couple since my wife stated early on that she didn't care for those kinds of activities. Several years later, something caught her and changed her feelings about it. In my early twenties I parachuted with a friend who was in a skydiving club. My wife was not fond of the idea. Years passed and she brought up, out of the blue, the idea of a hot air balloon ride. I heard what she said and I listened as well. We made that first trip and she loved it!

As we grow we change. Nothing stays the same forever. This includes people's thoughts and feelings about things. You have to be a good listener to know how this works. Some people will never do certain things, regardless of the circumstances. Others may not do something at first, but over time, they have the option to change. People can change in as little as a few days or take as long as a few decades. Your job is to pay attention. If you are unsure of something, then ASK! There are no dumb questions, only dumb guesses from someone who was afraid to ask.

# ATTITUDE

If you have "attitude" – lose it! Drop it, get rid of it! It will usually do you more harm than good. A great rule of thumb is, "Never take it personally." I'll recommend further reading in this area. A great resource has been provided by Don Miguel Ruiz in his book, "The Four Agreements." Agreement number two: Don't take anything personally. This is a great book to read if you want to become the best version of yourself. It sold over five million copies in over 30 languages. If you don't have time to read it, you can by the CD version. For under $20.00, this is a great investment to make for yourself.

Another way to look at your attitude is like this. If you had a daughter and she wanted to date someone, would you really want her to date someone like yourself? Honestly looking at who you are can open your eyes to positive changes.

# HYGIENE

I hesitated when writing this section because you would think that everyone should be aware of this. It's important to keep the body clean, as smells (especially dirty or unpleasant smells) can be a real turn off to others. No one wants to be near a person who smells like a locker room before shower time. A little soap and water will go a long way.

Oral care is necessary as well. When we speak with someone we project the odor (good or bad) from our mouth almost directly into their nose. If you brush your teeth or use a mouthwash or both, the projected smell is much more pleasant.

Wearing clean clothing is also a plus. It's not necessary to wear designer clothes (unless that is in your budget) but clothes that have been washed and look and smell nice will be appreciated by your honey.

I attended a week long seminar in California a few years ago. One of the projects we participated in was to be homeless for a day. We had to remove all our personal jewelry and trade our own clothing in for the clothing they had waiting for us. Some of it was ripped or torn, and although the clothes had been washed, some pieces had stains on them. We were taken downtown and the object was to get lunch by panhandling or whatever creative way we could obtain it.

I was quite embarrassed walking down the street in the clothing I was wearing. It was a little tight fitting, the shirt had a rip in it and the pants were stained. I passed a man on the street who was truly homeless. He looked at me and asked what I was doing. I stated I was trying to get food for lunch. He smiled and said, "You're not homeless!" I was quite surprised by this remark and asked him what he meant. He told me he had seen several other people walking around looking as I did and wanted to know if we were conducting an experiment of some kind. He told me to look at him; the clothing he was wearing was not stained or ripped. He said a homeless person would not wear clothing like I was wearing. They have places to go to obtain clean clothes that are not stained or torn. They have places to go to take hot showers and clean up. He then introduced me to a few other homeless people on the street. You would not believe that they were truly homeless. You can't judge a book by its cover but you can be clean about your appearance since many people will notice.

Aloha Heart

"To love is to be happy with,"
says the Aloha King.
" Yes," says my heart.

" That is it, exactly."

-Kanta Bosniak, from "Love Poems"

Use this space for notes, thoughts and your own ideas:

# BE PUNCTUAL

When you tell your honey that you will arrive at a certain time, be there at that time. Yes, now and then we have situations that happen. A car can get a flat tire, traffic can be horrible on a road if there is a breakdown up ahead and the list goes on. It pays to leave a few minutes early and take your time to arrive safely and comfortably.

If you have a dinner reservation, you need to honor that time as you may be asked to wait if you are late.  Concerts, plays, movies as well as trains and planes have a timetable to follow. If you are late, you may miss an event entirely. Avoid the hassle and arrive on time.

If you say you are going to call her, **make the call!** It is incredibly rude to tell someone that you will call them and then you don't.  If you have no intention of calling her back, be man enough to say so.

# COURTESY

Always be courteous in everything you do. This idea is meant to go beyond your own personal relationships. I learned several years ago that, "How you do anything is how you do everything." Think about how you do things in general.

I believe in equality between men and women; equal pay for equal work, job opportunities at all levels for both sexes, and all of these related ideas. This is fine and good, however, common courtesy should continue regardless. I will not only hold a door open for a woman, I'll hold it open for anyone coming out behind me, man, woman or child. This is common courtesy. I go the "extra mile" for my honey; I open the car door for her and I walk on the street or curb side when we are out and about.

Something else to think about is that it's great to be considerate when you are with your loved one, however, if you pay attention, be aware that your courtesy is not becoming an annoyance. Some women may insist on opening the door themselves or walking on the street side. It's best NOT to offend them by trying to force your politeness on them. Once again – PAY ATTENTION! When you are observant, it will save you a lot of headaches.

# ALLERGIES

Find out early on if your honey is allergic to anything. This can prevent a serious life or death situation later on in your relationship. If she is allergic to nuts, you obviously avoid getting anything for her with nuts in it. She might be allergic to wool so you should avoid buying her clothing made from wool. I have a friend who has a serious allergy to shell fish. Several of us were eating at a restaurant one evening and the waiter asked her to pass a plate to another friend sitting in the corner. On the plate were steaming shrimp and just the smell from the hot steam caused her lips to swell and she had to leave the table.

# BUYING GIFTS

When it's time to buy a gift, using your listening and paying attention skills comes in very handy. Choose a gift that is meant for your partner as a token of your feelings. If you are not sure, then ask! You can ask close friends or family members if your honey is in need of something, or if she desires something in particular. Remember, it's the thought that counts. The price of a gift should not matter; it's the gift itself that really counts. Never overextend yourself simply to try to impress someone. If a designer purse is out of your budget then that is an item that you should avoid. Love is about feelings and emotions and should never be attached to dollar signs.

When you are with your honey, pay attention! They may see someone or something and make a remark about it. These, often casually made remarks, are important to keep track of. You will learn what they like and what they don't like about just about anything. Note their preference on color, style, length, shape and all aspects of the items they like.

For additional ideas on gift buying you can check out more information here:

http://www.streetdirectory.com/travel_guide/2622/gifts_for_lov ed_ones/how_to_buy_the_perfect_gift_for_anyone.html

http://www.findgift.com/categories/hard-to-buy-for

http://www.uncommongoods.com

# WHO ARE YOU REALLY GETTING THE GIFT FOR?

You present your lover with two tickets to the major league baseball game as a gift (birthday, anniversary, holiday) - whatever. This is great if she is REALLY a fan. If YOU are the fan and she is not, this is a horrible way to give a gift. Look at what it says; I only think about myself and you don't matter. When you give a gift to anyone - make sure it is a gift they will truly appreciate and be able to use. It is so sad to see how many gifts are "recycled" at the holidays simply because someone failed to take the time to assess the gift/receiver. It's just a waste of time to buy a gift for the sake of having something to give.

When buying a gift, be sure it will be appreciated by the receiver. If your partner prefers to wear crew neck or turtle neck tops, it's really inappropriate to by a low cut top just to show off her cleavage. She will not feel comfortable wearing it out in public and you will strike out on her emotional scoreboard.

Before computers, shopping was really a "hands on experience. If I wanted to buy my honey a gift, I actually had to go to the store and get the gift myself. This may have meant a trip to the mall during rush hour traffic, in inclement weather, on my lunch hour, etc. If you know precisely what gift you want to buy in today's world, you can go online 24/7. This can save time, money, and lots of other potential headaches.  When buying online, some stores offer free shipping and there is no sales tax from out-of-state stores.

# WRAPPING GIFTS

Everyone likes to receive gifts. When you present your lover with a gift, take the time to wrap it nicely. Handing someone a gift out of a paper bag with the price tag still on is rather tacky. You show your lover how much you care when you plan ahead. Whether you buy the gift in person or order it online, plan ahead to make sure you have the gift in time to be given on the day you want to give it.

If you decide to wrap the gift yourself, you can buy wrapping paper at many stores: department stores, supermarkets, drug stores, card stores, etc. You can choose from many styles of paper - special occasions like birthday, anniversary, mothers or fathers day, Christmas, Hanukkah, etc. Wrapping paper also comes in a wide variety from simple solid colors to wild designs as well. Choose the paper to fit the occasion.

Start on a flat, clean surface like a table. Remove the price tag from the item you are about to wrap. If you have difficulty removing a tag that is glued on a box, you can use a piece of scotch tape. Simply stick it to the price tag and pull it off. You may have to repeat this process more than once to get the tag off, but it generally works well. If the price is printed on the package, use a marker pen to blot it out. Place the paper "print side" facing down and center the gift on the paper. Measure the paper to the item being wrapped to be sure you have enough paper to fit all around the item. As a rule, boxed items wrap much easier than open items. A teddy bear in a box wraps easier than with no box. Once you are sure you have enough paper, cut away the excess paper. Neatly fold the paper around the box and tape in place. If you are uncomfortable wrapping your gift, many stores (even online) offer gift wrapping either free or for an additional charge. A neatly wrapped gift will show that you care about details and it will be appreciated by your lover.

When you purchase your wrapping paper, be sure to look for matching ribbon and bows. Match the ribbon and bow color to a similar color that is in the wrapping paper. You can wrap the ribbon around the center of the box then twist it underneath the box and bring it up on the opposite sides. Next, tie the ribbon in the middle of the box and tape a matching bow over the tied ends. Many stores also sell "wrapping kits" that comes complete with paper, ribbon and bows.

You can attach a gift tag to the box or slip a card under the ribbon.

You can also buy gift bags. These are colorful bags, often with handles, that come in a variety of sizes to match the size of your gift. Simply place your gift on some tissue paper (also sold with gift paper and bags) and place the item in the gift bag with tissue paper slightly sticking out of the bag. It looks elegant and it is very easy to do.

Love is when he gives you a piece of your soul, that you never knew was missing.

-Torquato Tasso

Use this space for notes, thoughts and your own ideas:

I bought a gift for my wife at an upscale store who had white satin gift boxes and they used a wide silver elastic ribbon to keep the box closed. There was no need to wrap this box any further, but I felt it still needed something more. I was giving this gift to her later on that day and on the way home from the store, I stopped at a florist. I bought a single red, short stem rose and slipped it under the ribbon. The white satin box with a beautiful red rose held in place by the silver elastic ribbon was perfect!  You can be as creative as you want.

I once wrapped what I called the "surprise box." I bought my wife a pair of diamond stud earrings as a birthday gift.  I wrapped the small box from the jeweler very elegantly.  I placed the small wrapped box (we'll call this box number one) into a slightly larger box and wrapped the larger box as well. We'll now call this box number two. I placed box number two into a larger box (box number three) that left about four inches of space on each side of box number two. I filled this space with (unbuttered) popcorn (the eating kind, not the styrofoam chips used for packing) with box number two buried in the center. I then wrapped box number three. I placed box number three into a slightly larger box (number four) and wrapped number four. Box four was placed into a slightly larger box (number five). I placed a card with a long note I wrote on the inside on top of box number five). In the note I wrote something like .... "I spent my life digging for a treasure, and then I found you." Box five was wrapped and then placed in box number six. I wrapped box number six as elegantly as the rest.

When I presented my wife with the gift, I asked her if she thought she could guess what was inside. The final box size was about 28x24x24. While she provided many interesting guesses, I knew she'd never know until she opened all the boxes. It was delightful watching her face as she opened the first box. She saw the card and the "next" wrapped box under it. She read the note I wrote with a warm smile on her face. She opened the next box only to find another, then another still. Opening this box she discovered what seemed to be a box of popcorn! The look of confusion on her face was priceless! "I thought you loved popcorn," I said. "I like it, but I don't love it that much," was her reply. I suggested that since she didn't love her gift as much as I thought, she better dig deeper. Finding the next smaller box she began laughing out loud. When she opened the last little box and saw the half carat earrings, the look on her face let everyone know that my stunt was worth it.

For more information on wrapping gifts, you can check out the following WEB sites:

http://www.realsimple.com/holidays-entertaining/gifts/wrapping/creative-gift-wrapping-ideas

http://www.papyrusonline.com/wrap-and-bags.html

http://www.homemade-gifts-made-easy.com/gift-wrapping-techniques.html

# HOLDING HANDS

When you are out walking, regardless of where you are, it's a wonderful feeling to have your hand held.  Understand that this is a two way process. It's very different from the way your mother held you by the hand as you were forced to go on a shopping trip. Being pulled through the aisles in the department store or supermarket is not what I am referring to. It takes both partners to hold hands. Be the one to initiate it. It's a warm and gentle feeling. Notice how your fingers intertwine. You can gently and slowly move your fingers around your lover's fingers every now and then. Holding hands may seem so insignificant, but it is a very powerful way to show your feelings to your lover. It also shows the people around you that you are a couple with a connection.

Consider this:  when you are in bed at night (for those couples who are married or perhaps living together), have you ever held your lovers hand as you drifted off to sleep? The bond that you create is warm, gentle and filled with love. When you awake in the morning, you may not be holding hands any longer but falling asleep this way is quite special.

# FLOWERS

Most people enjoy flowers. Take note, if your lover has allergies, this may not be a good idea! If they enjoy flowers, you will have many possibilities. You can buy fresh cut flowers from a florist, supermarkets or street vendors. Even Costco and BJ's Wholesale Clubs sell flowers. Understand too, that the colors of flowers, especially roses have different meanings. Red roses usually signify love and passion. Yellow roses can signify friendship, although at one time they signified jealousy. White roses signify loyalty and sincerity. There are several colors to choose from and you can read more about this at your library or at several WEB sites such as:

http://www.proflowers.com/blog/rose-colors-and-meanings

http://www.promgirl.com/prom-guide/flowers/flower-colors

http://www.wisegeek.com/what-do-different-colors-of-roses-mean.htm

Flowers can be used to convey thoughts, feelings and emotions. When someone is not feeling well, a bouquet of bright, multicolored flowers can be delivered to cheer them up. When you feel bad or sorry for something you said or did, a bouquet of flowers can be given as part of an apology. When you wish to express your love for someone, a bouquet of red roses is a great way to show it. Please be aware, it is unnecessary to wait for a special occasion to give flowers. Why not have a bouquet of flowers delivered to your honey's job "just because?" It's a wonderful way to say, "I love you, and I'm thinking about you!"

There are many ways to present flowers to your lover. You can show up for your date (or simply arrive home if that's the case) with flowers in your hand. You can have them delivered to your lover's home or delivered to their place of business. When you send flowers, you have the option of enclosing a card. Florists (either the local florist in town or the one on the Internet) will offer you a selection of cards fitting for every occasion, even if there is no special occasion at all! Some examples of Internet florists are:

http://www.FTD.com

http://www.1800Flowers.com

http://www.teleflora.com

Understand that size does not always matter! You can send four dozen red roses to your lover and it's just as elegant and impressive to send one single rose in a bud vase. Using the latter example, you may want to enclose a card that simply states, "You are the only one in my life!" Again, the possibilities are endless.

A vase of fresh cut flowers whether it's placed on a table, a mantle, a dresser or anywhere in the home stimulates the senses. The colors, regardless if they are mixed or all solid colors, are a beautiful sight before the eyes. The fragrance they provide is pleasantly stimulating to the nose. The softness of the petals is a delight to touch. Flowers are always welcome in my home.

# SENDING CARDS

Shopping for a card to send your lover is easy provided you follow some basic rules. Whether the card will be delivered by snail mail or e-mail, it's important to send the correct message. Take the time to READ the card and what it says. If what is written in the card does not really apply to the recipient, it will not matter how beautiful the card is designed. I've read hundreds and hundreds of cards over the years and while many were beautiful to look at, the message I wanted to convey had to be correctly expressed in the card if I was going to buy it.

If the person receiving the card is new in your life, you'd avoid sending a card that might say, "As I look back over the time we've spent together." Make sure your thoughts are correctly expressed. Sometimes you'll go through dozens of cards but finding the BEST card for the occasion is worth it. Sometimes you'll be lucky enough to read in a card something that your lover has actually said or expressed. My honey has often remarked about having love in her heart. I recently found a card that mentioned "having love in your heart" and immediately bought it. It pays to read through several cards to find the best one for the occasion.

This is another way of showing how attentive you are.

If you are good with words, you can buy "blank cards." Find a blank with an appropriate design or picture on the cover. You can add your own thoughts and feelings inside. It's wise to write it all out on a piece of paper first and once you have said all that you want to say, you can edit your work if necessary and insert your message inside the card.

You can view many cards online (e-cards). This is a nice way of giving your honey a warm surprise in her mail box. Many e-cards are free and others have a price, check them out before you decide. Either way, you'll have a great selection to choose from. Some sites will let you custom design your own cards. If you are creative or artistic, this can be a great way to go.

Many cards can be viewed here:

http://www.123greetings.com

http://www.americangreetings.com

http://www.us.moo.com/products/greeting-cards.html

Being deeply loved by someone gives you strength, while loving someone deeply gives you courage

-Lao Tzu

Use this space for notes, thoughts and your own ideas:

## SURPRISE HER WITH CARDS

Everyone loves a surprise and so will your lover. Find the right card that expresses what you want to say. Place the card in a place where it will be easily found by your lover. My wife teaches and I've put them in her grade book so that she'll discover the card while at school. You can put cards in the car, under a pillow, on a desk, in a book, in the refrigerator, in a purse, in a back-pack, on the sink, taped to a mirror, in a briefcase, the possibilities are endless. Make sure it's a place that your lover will be utilizing on the day you want the card found.

To make the card even more of a surprise, you can put inside the card a check, cash, gift certificate, etc. I know my wife was having a lunch date with some of the teachers she works with. I hid the card in her lesson plan book and had put $20.00 inside. A little note I added stated, "Your lunch is on me today!" The surprise of finding a card creates a wonderful feeling for the recipient, letting them know you are "thinking" about them. Paying for her lunch was an added bonus. The warmth and good feelings you create when you do this is priceless.

# WRITING & POETRY

Thoughts are wonderful but they are also fleeting. Take the time to put your thoughts about your lover on paper. Let your lover know what you like about her. Express how you feel when you are with her as well as how you feel when you are away from her. Sometimes it's easier to put your thoughts and words on a piece of paper than to say them out loud. Think about the thoughts you are feeling in your heart and write them down.

If you want to be creative, write poetry for your lover. Poetry does not have to rhyme and there are different styles of poetry. You can check your local library to find books on writing poetry and different examples of poetry styles. Do a WEB search on the Internet on writing poetry. Some sites you will find include, but are not limited to:

http://www.poetry-online.org/

http://www.poewar.com/poetry-writing-tips/

http://www.dummies.com/how-to/content/writing-poetry.html

There are several sites and books in print you can access to help you learn to express your thoughts in written words for your lover to read and appreciate. When your lover reads something you wrote, it engages several of the senses and that makes it a very powerful experience. As they hold the paper in their hands, it engages their sense of touch. As they read the words, it engages their sense of sight. As they read the words and hear them in their mind, it engages their sense of hearing. If you choose to splash a few drops (only a few are necessary – don't soak the paper) of your cologne on the page, it engages her sense of smell.  This symphony of senses creates an incredible experience for your honey.

If you are not comfortable writing your own poetry, you can find something that was written by a published poet. Write the poetry down and tell your honey something like, "When I read this poem by Elizabeth Browning, it reminded me of you." Then either read the poem to her or let her read it.

# READING POETRY

You can find good books from several well know poets in the library or online. Browse through them and find poems that you feel express your own inner thoughts and ideas about love or your lover. Find a comfortable place where you can be together and read the poems right out of the book. You can be in the living room, the back yard, on a picnic, at the beach, on a raft or you can be almost anywhere and share your feelings with your honey. Some of the authors you might want to explore regarding love poetry are: Elizabeth Barrett Browning, Kanta Bosniak, Lord Byron or Christina Rossetti.

Create an atmosphere that is fitting to the poetry you want to share with your honey. If you are inside during the evening, you might like to have some candles lit to create a soft and warm feeling. If you are out in the yard or on a picnic, find a spot under a shady tree to read your poetry. In many cases, the atmosphere that you create will be just as important as the poetry you read. Pay attention to details.

# MUSIC

When you listen to music, do you actually listen to the lyrics or do you just focus on the sounds made from the instruments? Pay attention to what is really being said when you listen to music. You will learn what the artist is saying and then you can use that piece of music to express your feelings about the one you care about. You can either play the song from a CD or MP3 or hear it on the radio and remark, "You know, that is how I feel about you," or "Each time I hear that song, I think about you." You can present your lover with the CD or MP3 as a gift and simply say, "I want you to have this so you'll know what I am feeling (or thinking) about you each time I hear it. Music has a very powerful emotional affect on the listener. Make sure you listen to the entire piece and all the verses so you are aware of what is being said. Nice sentiments may be conveyed in the first few verses but then the mood might change to something violent or negative. You need to be fully aware that the gift you are giving is the gift you actually intended to give.

You can buy music online or at many music stores. The online stores allow you to download the music instantly (you will have to pay for most of these) to your computer or iPhone. You can get the exact music you desire and have it available to play when you need it.

Some places you might look are:

https://www.jamendo.com/en/search

https://itunes.apple.com/us/genre/music/id34

http://mp3.com

# DEDICATING LIVE MUSIC

There are several radio stations across the country where you can call in and request to have a song dedicated to your lover on the air. I've done this and it's very romantic.  A friend of mine was a DJ for a major East Coast station when I was dating. I'd call him and ask to have a particular song played in a time range, say between 8:00 and 8:30 pm. I'd be able to "set the stage" and be sitting comfortably listing to the station with my honey and then my dedication would come on. You have the best of both worlds, your lover gets to hear the song expressing your feelings or thoughts and it's "from you to her" presented live for all listeners to hear. The element of surprise is also a great way to let your honey know how you feel about her.

# ANOTHER SURPRISE

I will give you another example of how I surprised my wife with a gift. It was her birthday and we were having a small party at our house. My wife stayed home to prepare the food and one of her friends came with me to "pick up a few things from the store." I had actually bought the main part of her gift already and needed a reason to get out to pick-up the rest of it. Note: this is the only time we have ever allowed each other to "lie" about an event. I needed a way to get her gifts to keep them a surprise so I "lied" and said I had to pick up some additional party supplies.

The first stop was to a major department store to buy her a pair of satin pajamas. I remembered her saying she would love to have them and knew this would be an ideal gift. (Remember to pay attention when your honey makes a remark about something). I bought ecru colored satin pajamas with a light brown edge all the way around. They put the pajamas in a satin box with a silver elastic band around the box. It looked so nice I knew I would not have to wrap it.

Next stop was to the jewelers. When I want to buy good jewelry for my wife, I always use the same jeweler we have been going to for years. I trust Rene Doumeng with all my important purchases. From her engagement ring to an anniversary watch, I want to be sure I am getting quality merchandise. If your budget does not allow for this, you can do whatever you can afford to do. Remember, it's the thought that counts, not the price.

My wife has always wanted a real pearl necklace, nothing gaudy but something elegant for certain outfits she had. I had picked out a short, one strand necklace with graduated pearls. They were smaller on the ends and became somewhat larger as you got to the center of the necklace. Once outside, I opened the box with the pajamas and clipped the pearl necklace around the collar of the pajamas, right on top. It looked just as if she was wearing it already. On the way home as I passed a florist I had a last minute great idea. I went in and bought a short-stemmed red rose and slipped it under the silver elastic band that went around the box. It looked quite elegant and it was unnecessary to wrap it with paper.

At the party, I had her open the box very carefully to prevent the necklace from sliding off the neck of the pajamas. When she saw the necklace around the neck of the pajamas, the look on her face was priceless.  Seeing the look in her eyes and the smile on her face certainly made the effort worthwhile.

Use this space for notes, thoughts and your own ideas:

# HUGS

Hugs are a wonderful way to show your honey that you care. Hugs can be used in a variety of ways as well. First of all, a hug is a warm and simple embrace. It's not a bear-hug that a wrestler might give an opponent. Hugs should never be used as a cheap way to crush your honey's boobs against your chest. Doing that kills everything on the spot because any good intentions you might have had planned just flew out the window.

You can hug someone to show your love and gratitude for them being in your life. You can hug someone to say "hello" and you can hug someone to say "goodbye." When someone is upset or hurt, you can hug them to show that you care. When someone is sad or depressed, you can hug them to show that you feel for them. When we hug, we raise the body's levels of oxytocin and serotonin which elevates our mood and happiness.

When is a good time to give your honey a hug? Anytime! Hugs are very important and beneficial to the human body. When I see my honey looking perplexed, unhappy or confused, I simply say, "It's hug time," and wrap my arms around her. This changes her mood almost instantly.

# A SIMPLE BACK RUB

Usually at the end of the day or at any time during a stressful situation, the upper back muscles tense up and can become quite tight and sore. This can actually be caused by chest breathing which we tend to do when we are stressed. If you are aware that your lover is tense, offer her a simple back rub. You can even do this by walking up behind her and gently placing your hands on her shoulders and softly working your fingers into the area beneath your hands. DO THIS SOFTLY! She will let you know if she wants a firmer massage. If you start out too hard, you will only aggravate the already sore muscles and cause more discomfort. Working the muscles increases the circulation to the area and allows the muscles to relax. Spend a little time here, a ten second massage is only a tease and can be annoying. Remember to STOP, if you are asked to. You are not the one feeling the sensation, the other person is and if it is uncomfortable to her, you need to stop.

A good massage can be priceless and most enjoyable to the receiver. The basic anatomy of the human body prevents us from massaging our own backs but we can be extremely helpful to someone in distress. Remember to be very gentle at the start. If more pressure is required, your partner will ask you to do so. You can ask as well, "Am I doing this firmly enough for you?" Everyone is different, some people like it softly and some like it firm.  Give your partner what she wants and that is what it is all about.

# LEARN TO GIVE A MASSAGE

There are many books that will explain the different types of massages and how to properly do them. By learning a few, easy to master skills, you will be able to provide a relaxing experience for your lover. You will learn about the setting, body position and a variety of materials to use with the massage such as rubbing alcohol, lotion, oils, etc. You will learn to use your hands the best way to create a delightful and relaxing massage for your partner.

You can use your library, a local book store or an Internet book store such as:

http://www.amazon.com

http://www.barnesandnoble.com

http://www.booksamillioninc.com

# HOT OIL MASSAGE

One example of a massage is the hot (it's actually warm) oil massage. Place a large clean towel or sheet on your bed or on the floor (wherever it's comfortable for your partner). As your partner disrobes, you take a bottle or tube (everything comes in plastic these days) of massage oil and place it in a basin (or sink) of very warm water for about ten minutes. The warm water will warm the oil in the bottle or tube. You may also place a small amount of the oil in a small plastic or metal bowl and place the bowl into a basin or sink of warm water. Once again, you have many possibilities. If the oil is unscented you can mix a few drops of your lovers perfume or favorite scent with the oil before you apply it. Apply some of the oil to your hands and rub them together for a few seconds.

You may want to start with your partner's neck and shoulders. Have your lover lie face down and use another towel or sheet to cover the areas not being worked on.  This will prevent your partner from getting a chill. Gently begin to work your fingers into the muscles. Ask your partner how it feels. Ask if they would prefer it to be a softer or firmer massage and honor their request. NEVER use excessive pressure or you may cause injury to your lover. If you have decided to massage the entire back part of the body, slowly work your way down from the neck to the shoulders, the upper back, the lower back, the buttocks, the upper legs, the lower legs and then the feet. Take your time. If you spend just four to five minutes on each area, this will take about thirty to forty minutes to accomplish. Give your hands a rest for a few seconds every now and then. Stretch out your fingers and allow your own circulation to come back into your hands. A good massage can be rather tiring for the average person's hands.

# REFLEXOLOGY

Reflexology is the art of foot massage. A good foot massage can take fifteen to thirty minutes for each foot! This is an extremely relaxing experience, especially if she has been on her feet all day at work. Once again, there are several books (and schools) available that explain reflexology and how different areas on the body correspond to different areas on the bottoms of your feet. Done properly, reflexology is very relaxing. Please note, for the person who has very sensitive feet, you will need to take care. The bottoms of many people's feet are very ticklish. What might start out as a great intention can turn out to be torture for someone with sensitive feet. If you learn to master reflexology correctly, you will be able to provide a relaxing experience that will be greatly appreciated.

Some guides that will help you learn this art are located at:

http://www.how-to-do-reflexology.com/

http://www.amazon.com/Feet-First-Guide-Foot-Reflexology/dp/0671634127

http://www.naturalhealthcourses.com/reflexology.htm

# CANDLES ADD AMBIANCE

The use of candles can be very romantic when used at the dinner table, during a bath, reading poetry and you have many other possibilities as well. Candles come scented (with a scent) or unscented (no scent). The scented candles come in dozens of delightful aromas - vanilla, berry, pumpkin pie, lavender, chocolate chip cookie dough, rose, apple cinnamon, blueberry muffin, coconut and the list goes on and on. If you choose to light several candles, keep one thing in mind. Choose a scent or two that seem to go well together. Too many different "smells" may be unpleasant or confusing to the senses. You may choose to have one or two scented candles and the others may be unscented.

Candles can be used for a soft lighting effect as with a candle-lit dinner. Two candles placed on the dinner table add a warm and pleasant touch. With the rest of the lighting either off or down low, candles provide a pleasant and warm way to illuminate your space. They can be used to add a delightful aroma (if scented) to the area as well. A single apple - cinnamon candle placed safely on a kitchen counter will fill the house with a delicious aroma as if someone just baked a pie. One

Thanksgiving my wife lit a pumpkin pie candle and everyone who visited wanted to know when we had time to bake the pie. Candles can be used as a warm background effect. A candle lit on a mantle or a shelf in the back of a room adds a very comfortable feeling to a room. The dim light, the soft flicker of the flame on the wick and even the small shadows cast can be very romantic.

Please remember that a candle is a burning fire and to keep them in a safe place. Curtains, drapes, paper and a host of other items can ignite and cause a terrible fire from a single candle flame. Candles can be accidentally knocked over and create a disaster. Always remember – safety first!

Love is a canvas furnished by nature and embroidered by imagination.

—Voltaire

Use this space for notes, thoughts and your own ideas:

# A HOT BATH

After a day at work (please remember for those who have children, being a stay-at-home mom is a full-time job), taking a long, hot, relaxing soak in the tub is a wonderful way to unwind. Simply add some bath oil or bath melts to comfortably warm water in the tub. You can do this for your honey as extravagantly as you like. You can use the bathroom as-is or add candles, flowers, music and any creative ideas you might have.

You can purchase bath oils or melts locally at a pharmacy or department store or visit some of these WEB sites:

http://www.aromaweb.com/articles/aromatherapybaths.asp

http://www.lushusa.com

http://www.bathandbodyworks.com

# BUYING CLOTHES FOR YOUR HONEY

Buying clothes for another person can be a little tricky. You need to learn a few basics to help you make the "better" choices. Know what size you need to buy. Yes, if it's the wrong size you can always take it back. However, your honey may have her heart set on the style and color you brought home and if you have to exchange it, the shop may not have the same color or style in stock. We do not intend to disappoint! If you are unsure of size, try to get a peak at a label on a similar article of clothing your honey already has. If you intend on buying jeans, check out a pair of jeans she already owns. Please understand something when buying clothing. Different manufactures are not always exactly the same when it comes to making clothing. A size eight jean from Gloria Vanderbilt may fit "differently" than a size eight Levi's. A medium blouse from Kenneth Cole may fit differently than one from J. Crew. Many times you can ask a knowledgeable sales assistant if the size on a particular item from a particular company is true to size.

Now it's time for color. You need to know two things about color. First, you need to know what colors your honey likes and dislikes. She may love coral but hate chartreuse (a bright, light green.) For help with different color choices, you can visit these WEB sites for more information:

http://www.thechicfashionista.com/your-best-perfect-colors.html

http://www.collegefashion.net/fashion-tips/how-to-find-your-perfect-colors

http://www.corporatefashionista.com/everything-you-need-to-know-about-decoding-falls-hottest-color-combos

If you buy an item of clothing (such as a blouse), you need to either match it to something your honey already has or consider buying matching pants or skirt to go with it. To assist you in matching colors, check out the following WEB sites:

http://www.jurgita.com/articles-id2117.html

http://www.chiff.com/a/fashion-colors.htm

http://www.cosmopolitan.com/style-beauty/fashion/advice/a5759/simple-ways-to-master-color-mixing/

There are two tests you must make when you buy clothing. The first test is the well-made test. Look inside the clothing at one of the seams. This is the area where two pieces of material are sewn together. Count the number of stitches there are in one inch of the seam. If there are less than eight, the clothing is made cheaply. If there are more than eight, the clothing is of a better quality and will be stronger and last longer. Remember, you buy cheap, you get cheap. The more stitches per inch, the stronger the clothing will be.  There are some exceptions here, but I am not a tailor and I think you should get the general idea from what I said.

This next test is the one I love to do. If you decide you have the right size, the right style, the right color and more than eight stitches per inch, you now check on how the material will hold up while being worn. Take the material (the arm, leg, anywhere) and grasp it with both hands. Firmly twist the material in your hands and hold for about ten to fifteen seconds. When you let go, does the material relax back into shape or does it hold the wrinkles you just produced? If it holds the wrinkles, you know that after wearing it for fifteen or twenty minutes and sitting in the car, you'll look like you slept in it all night. If the material relaxes back into shape when you let it go, most likely it will look good on you a few hours later as well.

Shoes are a different story altogether. I would never buy my wife a pair of shoes if she was not present in the store with me. While we do not necessarily "feel" clothing that we are wearing, we stand in our shoes much of the day and we MUST be comfortable in them. There are too many styles, types of materials, designs and colors from which to choose. If you really want to score big points with your honey, offer to go shopping for shoes with her!

My wife has a very unusual foot size, a 10 AAA. It can be very difficult to buy shoes for her. I know this for a fact as I have gone with her on several occasions. She dislikes a narrow toe shoe as it cramps her toes and is very uncomfortable for her. She prefers a shoe with soft leather that fits well. It's almost funny; one of the few places that we have found shoes that fit her very well was in Paris, France. Almost every store we visited had comfortable shoes in her size, but that's one heck of a commute to buy shoes!

# COOK A MEAL

Cooking is not only for women. Some of the best recipes come from the firehouses in New York City. There are several cook books written by firemen from around the country.

Even if you've never really boiled water before, it's easy to prepare a meal for your lover that will be easy and impressive. Remember, it's the thought that counts. A delicious Italian dinner is only minutes away! What you'll need: a small box of spaghetti (the pasta of your choice), (or container of refrigerated pasta), a jar of good pasta sauce or clam sauce, a small loaf of Italian bread, small jar of grated cheese, bottle of wine (not always necessary, it depends on your taste).Two long, slim candles in holders set on your table will add a great touch. If you decide to buy a bottle of wine and are new at this, go to your local liquor store and ask about the different varieties of wine that would go well with a spaghetti dinner. Your wine merchant will explain about different types of wine - dry, sweet, etc. You can also go to the following WEB sites and educate yourself about wine:

www.winemag.com/wine-for-beginners

http://winefolly.com/wine-basics-beginners-guide

http://www.npr.org/blogs/thesalt/2014/02/07/272515201/wine-wisdom-with-a-wink-a-slackers-guide-to-selecting-vino

A nice red wine goes well with a spaghetti dinner. Red wines run from sweet to dry, depending on your taste. First, set the table with two of each: plates, forks, knives, spoons, napkins and wine glasses (if you are having wine).  Next, place the candle holders in the center of the table about eighteen to twenty-four inches apart. (Light them last, just before you serve the cooked meal). Follow directions on the package of spaghetti and make enough for two servings. Boil the water and add the spaghetti as directed on the box or package.

Half way through the cooking time, put two servings of sauce in a small pot and heat under low flame, stirring every now and then. Do not heat too fast or over a high flame. Cut the bread into one inch slices but not all the way through, leave a little crust on the bottom to hold it together. When the spaghetti is done, put the bread, wrapped in a paper towel in the microwave for about 30 - 40 seconds and warm it, a little longer if you use a toaster oven. Add the sauce to the top of the spaghetti and serve.  Pour the wine of your choice into stemmed glassware and enjoy. Turn down the lights and enjoy a romantic candle-lit dinner! The cooking and prep time for this meal is less than 40 minutes and quite easy to do. Show your honey how you love her with a home-cooked meal!

# TAKE HER OUT TO BREAKFAST, LUNCH OR DINNER

If you are truly afraid that you'd be all thumbs in a kitchen and cannot fathom the thought of preparing a meal, take her out to eat! The best way to discover who your lover is and what she likes is by asking questions. When she speaks, remember to LISTEN! What kind of food does your lover enjoy? There are many types of restaurants in larger cities: American, French, Italian, Irish, Chinese, German, Spanish, Thai and the list goes on and on. If you decide on taking your honey out to dinner, pick a place where she will enjoy the food. We have several restaurants that we enjoy as well as several types of food.  We even enjoy a local diner that has a pleasant and relaxing atmosphere.

Another thought you need to consider is the price range of the restaurant you choose. Understand that the quality of the food served does not necessarily go up if the price goes up. I've seen restaurants serve sad, skimpy meals for over $90.00 a person. I've also seen a $12.00 lunch with so much good food, you either had to share with someone or take half of the meal home. You may have also seen restaurants with a "prix fixe" menu.

This is a French term and it means that there is a "fixed" or set price for a meal. Always be aware of the cost of eating at a restaurant before you make a reservation. Many years ago when I was in college, a few friends got together to go out to eat. One guy recommended a nice place that he had been to recently with his family. We inquired about the cost and he said it was "average." After we were seated, (there was no menu in the window) we finally got to see the menu and the cost was about three times the money we had on us. We had to politely get up from this crowded establishment simply stating to the waitress that there was nothing on the menu that was interesting to us.

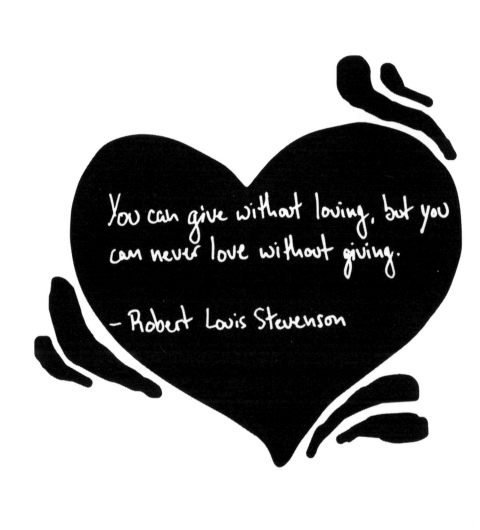

You can give without loving, but you can never love without giving.

- Robert Louis Stevenson

Use this space for notes, thoughts and your own
ideas:

Restaurants receive ratings that you can review to decide if you might want to explore a particular establishment.  These ratings will give you a lot of information about the particular restaurant such as hours of business, menus, price range, atmosphere, dress code and more. You can read reviews of restaurants in your local newspaper or visit the following WEB sites:

http://www.zagat.com

http://www.tripadvisor.com/Restaurants

http://www.wikihow.com/Find-a-Great-Restaurant

# BAKE A CAKE

It's easier to make a cake than you might think. It might be for a birthday, an anniversary or no reason in particular, but your honey will be delighted that you took the time to do this. ONE WORD of caution, you may wish to avoid baking a cake if your sweetie is in the process of losing weight. Never do anything that might seem as if you are sabotaging your honey.

The quick and simple way is making a cake from a mix. You may want to decide on a bundt cake which often requires no fancy frosting on top. You'll need a bundt pan, the mix and a few additional ingredients listed on the back or side of the box. Follow the directions and in less than ninety minutes, you have a delicious surprise for your lover.

If you are a little more experienced (or daring - lol), you may decide to make a cake from scratch. Remember, your honey will not only appreciate the delightful dessert you prepared, she'll love the thoughtfulness and effort you put into it by making it by yourself. Check out the following WEB sites for easy to bake cake recipes:

http://allrecipes.com/Recipe/Simple-White-Cake/Detail.aspx

If you want to really surprise your lover, make a cake in the afternoon and surprise her with it as dessert after the dinner you cooked above! You say so very much without opening your mouth when you take the time to do something special for the one you love.

I'll share a simple recipe for making a white cake that is very impressive. (Just a note: when I was in college, I used to bake cakes and sell them to restaurants. I made some nice money doing this).

It will take about 40 minutes to put this together and about 35 minutes to bake the cake.

**You will need the following:**

2 ¼ cups of sifted flour

1 1/3 cups of sugar

3 teaspoons of baking powder

½ cup of butter – softened

½ teaspoon of salt

¾ cup of milk

2 teaspoons of vanilla extract

4 egg whites (you can substitute two tablespoons of eggbeaters for each egg white needed)

**Preparation:**

 Preheat your oven to 350 degrees. Grease (use a spray or butter or margarine) then dust with flour, the inside of a 13" x 9" pan. Line the bottom with a piece of waxed paper.

Sift the flour, sugar and baking powder in a large mixing bowl. Add the butter, the salt, the milk and the vanilla.  Beat at a low speed until blended. Beat on a medium speed for about two minutes and remember to scrape the sides of the bowl. Add the unbeaten egg whites and beat for another two minutes on the medium speed.

Pour the batter into the 13" x 9" pan and bake at 350 for about 35 minutes. The top should be a light golden brown, the sides of the cake will be slightly pulling away from the pan and if you insert a toothpick into the center, it will pull out clean (no batter sticking to it). Let the cake cool completely and turn the pan over while holding a wire (or cooling) rack (a plate will do as well) over it.

The frosting is easy – you can buy a prepared frosting and spread it right out of the can, or make the homemade frosting I have added below.

**VANILLA FROSTING:**

3 cups of confectioners' sugar

¾ cup of butter (softened)

1 teaspoon of vanilla extract

1 to 2 tablespoons of milk

In a mixing bowl, add the sugar and the butter and mix on low speed till blended. Continue mixing on a medium speed for another 3 to 4 minutes. Slowly add the milk until the frosting is easily spreadable, being careful to avoid getting it too watery.

To make a chocolate frosting, simply add 2/3 cup of cocoa powder with the sugar (as above) and increase the milk to 3 – 4 tablespoons to make it creamy and spreadable.

If a cake seems too complex, you can make cupcakes! Place paper cupcake liners in a cupcake pan and fill each one about 2/3 full of batter. Bake the cupcakes about 15 to 20 minutes, until an inserted toothpick comes out clean.

Making a cake or even cupcakes for your honey will be a real surprise. You are coming from your heart and doing something that will always be remembered.

# WALKING

Walking with your partner is a simple way to share time together. There are a few basics to follow but they are easy to master. When a male is walking with a female, he should be on the outside or curb side of the sidewalk or walkway. This is a way to insure safety for the female. When you are walking you can either hold hands or have your arms around each other, which ever you are most comfortable with. In the event that you have done some shopping and you are carrying the packages for her, you may not be able to hold hands at all.

As you are walking with your partner pay attention to how fast she moves. It is rude to be moving so fast that you are dragging your partner around with you. The idea is to comfortably be walking together, whatever the pace. As long as you are keeping up with each other, that will work fine.

Walking gives you time to both explore and communicate. While it is necessary to pay attention to where you are walking, the attention required is not as great as when you are driving. If you desire a walk for a relaxing chat with each other, you have many options. You might choose the boardwalk at a local beach, a path through a park, the grassy edge around a beautiful lake, through a flower garden at an arboretum, down a small street filled with restaurants, even in the local mall! I know of couples who go window shopping at the mall on a regular basis. The exercise is great, there is usually security in the mall for safety, the mall air temp is controlled for comfort and they might even buy a few items as well.

Please keep in mind that there is a time and a place for everything. While walking can be very relaxing and romantic, make sure she is wearing shoes that are meant for walking. If she is wearing heals, a long walk is not actually a great idea. Comfortable shoes work best for a good walk.

There is only one kind of love, but there are a thousand imitations.

-Francois de La Rochefoucauld

Use this space for notes, thoughts and your own ideas:

# FUN THINGS THAT COUPLES CAN DO TOGETHER

Are you tired of the same old, same old? Look at new and adventurous things you can do with your honey for fun. Remember, when you are with someone you care about, anything can be fun when doing it together as long as you both have an interest in what is being done. That is the key phrase here "both having an interest" in the event. Inviting your honey over to help you change your oil or clean out the garage is not really most people's idea of having fun together. Don't get me wrong, this can be an adventure as long as **both parties** feel that way.

You need to be considerate of your partner's feelings, fears, thoughts about things, etc. If your sweetie is petrified of snakes, a visit to the reptile house at the zoo is not a good idea. If she has a fear of heights, going on a rollercoaster ride or skydiving doesn't work either. You should be getting the idea here. If either of you has a particular like that the other has no interest in or desire to try, never force the issue. My wife loves to fly in planes but she has no desire to jump out of them. When I suggested skydiving, she smiled and said, "You go and have a wonderful time, I'll have more fun staying home." I went with friends and did it on my own. We simply agreed to disagree on how much fun that activity would be.

It's a different story if you both agree to try something that is new to one or both of you. If you both like swimming and the water in general, learning to scuba dive might be a good idea. If you like rides that move fast and go up high, trying the new rollercoaster at an amusement park is OK too.

If you find that you're spending every night glued to the television set, it's time for a change. You need to try new things so get out and have some fun!

# LEARN TO DANCE

Dancing is fun, great exercise and a way to have physical (non-sexual) contact with your partner. Many times we have been out and saw the same thing: guys standing around talking while the women were dancing with each other. If you do not know how to dance, NOW is a great time to learn. Whether you are single or a couple, you can take dancing lessons. If you're single and learn to dance, you will always be ready when the music starts playing. If you are a couple already, it will be a wonderful experience for both of you. Your honey will be pleased and happy that you are willing to do this. The fun you both have on the dance floor will be priceless.

There are many ways to learn to dance. If you have a partner who is a good dancer, have them teach you. A CD or iPod with an external speaker will do the trick. Make the time to learn and be sure to LISTEN. Remember that practice makes perfect. I have friends who learned to dance from their mother, sister, cousin and the possibilities are endless.

If you feel embarrassed dancing with a family member, you have several other possibilities as well. Look in the adult education booklet from your local school district. You can check with adult education at local or community colleges too. Some communities offer programs like dancing through local parks or community centers. If all else fails, check your local phone book under the listing for "dance instruction." You can find free dancing instructions on the internet as well. Look for dance instruction on YouTube.com. Be aware that the cost goes up as you move from internet lessons or adult education classes to private, professional instruction at a studio.

You can check the following WEB sites for more information:

http://www.learntodance.com

http://www.fredastaire.com

http://www.arthurmurray.com/index.htm

# LEARN A NEW LANGUAGE TOGETHER

This is actually a fun activity, especially if you plan to visit a foreign country where they speak a language other than your own. I studied French in school and my wife studied Spanish. It was amazing that we found ourselves in Germany one vacation and we did not know any German, well, very little at best. The concept here is doing an activity together, not for competition, but just for the fun of it. You can practice with each other at home (when you don't want the kids to know what you are saying), or when you are out at a restaurant. Try going to a restaurant whose origin is a country that speaks the language you are learning and order your food. When you have your new language basics down, you can go to see foreign films for practice and even many DVD's come in a choice of languages. Watch your favorite movie in your new language.

Learning a new language can be done in several ways. You can purchase CD language courses from bookstores or online. You can look into local adult-education programs (high schools and colleges) for beginning language courses. You can enroll in for-credit courses in local colleges and take beginning, intermediate and advanced lessons. You can also learn from language schools that offer private and group instruction. Check your local phone book or visit the following WEB sites for more information on learning a new language:

http://www.language-learning-advisor.com

http://www.rosettastone.com

http://www.berlitz.us

# TAKE A KAYAK TRIP

If you enjoy being on the water, this is a great way to have fun in the warmer weather. Please do not confuse a kayak trip with a wet and wild white water rafting trip. While you can take a kayak into some very turbulent water, this is not what I am referring to. Kayak trips can be done on lakes, in rivers or streams and we have even kayaked in the ocean. These trips can last from an hour or two up till several days. The possibilities are almost endless.

Our first kayak trip was on a tidal river and took about 2 ½ hours. The trip was synchronized with the tide. If the tide was coming in, you started near the opening by the ocean and if the tide was going out, you started at a park way up stream. My honey does not swim, but thought a kayak trip would be fun. Everyone is asked to wear a life vest for safety. The tide moved at about 2 to 2.5 miles per hour which was not very fast at all. The big job was to steer the kayak with the paddle and keep it away from the banks of the river, which is fairly easy to do. In some places the water was about fifteen feet deep and in other places it was about fifteen inches deep. In some places the river was about 150 feet wide and in others it was about 12 feet wide. The trip took a little over two hours as we zigzagged up the river.

The scenery was beautiful and the adventure was very relaxing. We packed a simple lunch and enjoyed a relaxing, smooth trip. We saw lots of wildlife along the way from the fish in the water to geese, swans, raccoons, rabbits, and several other small animals.

For more information about kayak trips see these WEB sites:

http://www.paddling.net/trips

http://www.canoekayak.com

http://www.wavelengthmagazine.com

# PICNICS

If you've never been on a picnic, you need to try it at least once. A picnic can be for a group of family members and friends or an intimate little event for just the two of you. You can make it as simple or as elegant as you desire. Pack your favorite foods and beverages in a cooler and go to a park, beach, scenic overlook or anywhere you want to go. Your picnic can be a little fancy as well. You can buy wicker picnic baskets that come with plates, silverware and even stem ware. There is also room for food and a bottle of wine. Decide on what you want to eat and either prepare it yourself or call your local catering shop or delicatessen and place the order. Bring along a blanket and have a great time.

The items you can bring on a picnic are endless. You can take hot soup, cold chicken, sandwiches of any type, salads, meats, veggies, pickles, wine, lemon aid, bottled water and the list goes on. Be sure to consider what your honey enjoys eating and the best way to pack those foods for the picnic.

See the following WEB sites for more picnic ideas:

www.designmom.com/2013/06/living-well-12-secrets-for-the-perfect-picnic

http://www.realsimple.com/holidays-entertaining/entertaining/everyday-celebrations/picnic-packing-checklist

http://www.canadianliving.com/food/entertaining/how_to_plan_the_perfect_picnic.php

Friendship is love without his wings!

– Lord Byron

Use this space for notes, thoughts and your own ideas:

# TAKE A DAY TRIP

Day trips away are fun and you can arrange them to be as simple or as wild as your imagination allows. What does your honey enjoy? If your sweetie loves art or antiquities, you can spend hours browsing through a local museum.  Take a break for lunch at a local eatery and return to view the masters. Is your honey more of an outdoor type?  Visit a near-by town or state park and explore the hiking trails. This may be a good opportunity to have that "picnic" as described in another section.

Take the time to learn what your honey finds interesting and show that you want to share those interests as well. Many of the sections that are mentioned here can be turned into day trips. Kayaking, picnics and cruises can all be delightful day-long adventures. Use your search engine and put in the phrase "Day Trips" and you'll get several ideas for exciting day trips in your area.

# WEEKEND OR OVERNIGHT TRIPS

You may want to surprise your honey with an overnight trip. You may know of a hotel or cabin tucked away in the woods by a beautiful lake. It might be a ski lodge up in the mountains or an overnight cruise to nowhere. If you both enjoy roughing it a bit, a camping trip might be the thing to do. Just getting away from the same old, same old can be very relaxing and your honey will appreciate you for it.

Please keep in mind, if you are planning to take your honey away from it all, you really need to emphasize the "away from it all" part. If you are going camping, your honey should be there to relax, NOT to set up the tent, cook the food, clean the dishes, etc. She would have preferred to stay home and do all that in the comfort of her familiar surroundings. If you search the internet for "overnight trips," you'll get thousands of possibilities to choose from.

# BED AND BREAKFAST TRIPS

If you've never been to a bed and breakfast (B & B), you're missing a lot of fun. Most B & B's are homes that have been converted to accommodate guests. We have stayed in a few different B & B's and found them to be warm, friendly and delightful. In most B & B's, the name says it all - you get the bed (your private room) and your breakfast in the morning. Lunch and dinner are on your own, usually at a local eatery. Many B & B's are old houses that have been refurbished into beautiful homes. Some owners have taken a great deal of time and energy acquiring antique furnishings to compliment the time period of the house. When you walk into your room, it will seem as if you went through a time warp into a past century. We've met friendly people, some of whom we've stayed in touch with to this day.

For more information and locations of B & B's, see the following WEB sites:

http://www.bedandbreakfast.com

http://www.bedandbreakfastcenter.com/partners.cfm

http://www.balloonbedandbreakfast.com

# LONGER TRIPS

If your honey enjoys traveling, find out what kind of adventures she likes. Do you enjoy going where there are lots of people around or do you prefer the quiet, out of the way places? If you are going to a new destination for the first time, you need to do a little checking first. What time of the year are you planning your trip? Many places have rainy seasons and you'd find yourself ankle deep in mud if you go at the wrong time. Other countries have their summers and winters at different times than yours does. Is a different language (from yours) spoken in the destination you want to visit? What type of currency is used? Can you safely drink the water at your destination? Is the destination you desire to visit a SAFE place to visit at this time? One of the best ways to prepare for a longer trip is by dealing with a reputable travel agent. Your travel agent can advise you of all the above and lots more. Remember, ASK questions. The more information you have, the more comfortable you will feel about your trip.

For more information about travel, visit the following WEB sites:

http://travel.state.gov

http://www.woodburytravel.com

http://www.cbsnews.com/sections/travelguru/main502043.shtml

# HOT AIR BALLOON RIDE

Sometimes just doing something different can be a lot of fun and it demonstrates some creativity on your part. Doing something "different" or something your friends or family have never done can be very exciting. Remember, "There is a FIRST time for everything." I remember my wife remarking during a T.V. commercial that "I would love to do that one day." As I entered the room I could see several hot air balloons floating through the sky on the T.V. "Are you really serious," I asked her. She said she had always thought about it and to see it here, it looked so romantic. I filed that thought in the back of my head and made a note in my calendar as her birthday was in July, just three months away.

A hot air balloon ride is fun, relaxing and exciting as well. Even if you are afraid of heights or flying in general, you can still have a wonderful experience in a hot air balloon. Professional balloon pilots usually will not fly if the weather is bad or the winds are more than 10 - 12 miles per hour. If the winds are too strong the balloon will fly too far out of the local area. Remember, balloons are easier to control up and down than sideways since you fly with the air currents. As you move higher in the sky, the currents can change direction and skilled pilots can use this to help direct the balloon. The balloon pilot stated that even people who dislike airplanes or who get nervous with heights can enjoy a ride in a hot air balloon.

Most balloon flights are either starting at sun up or ending near sun down. I have taken a few flights and all have been in the morning. You will need to get up very early for this flight as you must be at the airfield at sun up! We traveled about two and a half hours upstate the day before and checked into a hotel. We were up at 4:30 am to shower, dress and have a quick bite to eat before we left for the airfield. After a short ten minute drive we were there.

The pilot and crew met the eight adventurers who would travel this morning in two different balloons. There was a nice mix of people from several different locations and backgrounds as well. None of us ever took this kind of trip before. We were all novices. You could volunteer to help inflate the balloon if you wished. The pilot gave out heavy work gloves to the volunteers and in short order, the balloon was ready to go.

The passengers climbed into the wicker basket and off we went. It was absolutely amazing! The balloon rose so calmly and quietly, you really did not feel it moving. It was as if the scenery in front of you was moving instead. Everyone's cameras began clicking away. The hour long ride was incredible. The pilot showed us points of interest as we flew by and we even passed the hotel in which we spent the night. When it was time to land, the pilot found a large field where he set the balloon down. After we packed up the balloon, we had a champagne toast, as is customary with most flights.

For more information on hot air ballooning, you can check these WEB sites:

http://www.balloonbedandbreakfast.com

http://www.hotairballooning.com

http://www.hotairballoons.com

# RENT A LIMO

You can rent a stretch limo for a day trip for just the two of you! A stretch Lincoln Town car in the New York area will cost about $500.00 for a six hour rental. Different locations as well as different sizes and types of vehicles will affect the pricing. Pick a destination about an hour and a half to two hours away. You can bring your own food, drinks and music and party along the way! Playing your honey's favorite music while you sip a glass of wine or champagne in the back of a limo is quite romantic. Try having your honey nibbling on chocolate covered strawberries as you give her a foot massage! After you arrive at your destination, have that picnic lunch as mentioned in another section of this book. On that ride back home, you have the peace and quiet to express your love for the one you love! Just remember to have the chauffeur close the privacy window. You can check your local phone directory or newspaper for information on limo rentals in your area. Call a few different numbers and compare the information.

I give you a box
tied with a shiny ribbon,
all my love inside.

— Kanta Bosniak, from "Sacred Love"

Use this space for notes, thoughts and your own ideas:

# SLOWER TRAVEL -

# TAKE A WALKING TOUR

Traveling by foot is both relaxing and good for your cardiovascular system as well. When you drive your car, and many people take the car one block down the road to get a newspaper or a container of milk, you miss so much of what is going on around you. We enjoy going for walks and have done so in many places. We live in a nice neighborhood and we can take a two mile round trip walk any time of the day or night. When you walk, you get to see so much more of what is going on around you. You notice trees, flowers, the design of a neighbor's garden, styles of homes and so much more that you really do not see when driving by in a car. Walking this way gives you a chance to talk with your honey about things we seem to never have the time to talk about otherwise. Remember to turn off your cell phone and enjoy your time together.

You can walk at the beach or a lake, a community or state park and many people even walk at the mall. We prefer quieter settings so we are generally outside for walks.  Some parks have outdoor cardio stations that you can walk through.

Each stop along the way gives you instructions for different cardio workouts. Walking down the beach or at a lake at either sunrise or sun set is absolutely beautiful.

If you're in the mood for something with more mental stimulation, almost every large city offers dozens of different walking tours. You can explore architecture, restaurants, historic sites, old mansions, museums, take ethnic eating tours and the list goes on.

Some ideas for walking tours can be found at:

http://www.bigonion.com

http://www.chicagotraveler.com/tour-chicago-by-walking.htm

http://www.denver.org/things-to-do/itineraries/denver-architectural-treasures

# PROFESSIONAL MASSAGE

In the event that you find giving a good massage too physically tiring, or due to medical reasons you are unable to give a massage (such as arthritis or other reasons), you can always locate a day spa or a massage therapist in your area and give your lover a gift certificate. Massage professionals are both male and female and you'll need to decide which gender you are the most comfortable with. Massage professionals are highly ethical and very well trained. I've had professional massages and they were extremely enjoyable. The cost can vary depending on your location and the length of time of the massage. To locate a licensed professional massage therapist in your area, check your local yellow pages, call the local chamber of commerce, or do a search on the Internet. You can also arrange for a couples massage where you both have a massage at the same time with two massage therapists.

www.massagetherapy.com

http://online.wsj.com/news/articles/SB10001424052702304537904577277303049173934

http://www.naturaltherapypages.com.au/article/what_is_relaxation_massage

# PROFESSIONAL REFLEXOLOGY

Reflexology is the art of foot massage. A good foot massage can take up to thirty minutes for each foot! This is quite a relaxing experience and you can gift it to your partner or do it together as a couple. Check your local phone directory or the internet for places to visit for professional reflexology. Many places that perform massage work will also do reflexology. A trained therapist will work with you to provide a comfortable experience.

You can explore these WEB sites for more information:

http://www.reflexology-usa.net/facts.htm

http://altmedicine.about.com/od/therapiesfromrtoz/a/Reflexology.htm

http://www.mayoclinic.org/healthy-living/consumer-health/expert-answers/what-is-reflexology/faq-20058139

# BICYCLE RIDING AND TRIPS

If you both have bikes and know how to ride, a bike trip can be a fun and relaxing way to enjoy a day with your honey. Many areas have bicycle trails to guide you safely on your journey. You can combine more than one of the ideas in this book to create a perfect day. Take a bicycle trip to the beach or a lake. Pack a picnic lunch to take along with you. This is another way to enjoy scenic views of the area combined with a great way to promote good health.

Bicycle tours can be as simple as half day trips in your local area or you can take week long (and longer) trips in other countries. If you have the time and the desire to do something off the beaten path, this is a great way to go. You can choose from beginner tours for the novice to extensive trips for the experienced cyclist.

http://www.backroads.com

http://www.adventurecycling.org/guided-tours

http://www.duvine.com

# ADULT EDUCATION CLASSES

Maybe there is a new hobby or computer course or any area of interest that you'd like to learn more about. Learning something new together can be a fun way to spend time with your honey. Adult education classes offer you dozens of programs to choose from and usually at convenient times. The fees for these classes are usually quite reasonable and sometimes even free for area residents. You can learn photography, drawing, painting, sculpting, how to play musical instruments, computer programs, stress management and relaxation, writing classes, fitness classes, sports programs and the list is endless. Most of these classes are noncredit and last from eight to twelve weeks.

Please contact your local school district or community college for more information on adult education classes.

# LEARNING HOW TO REALLY RELAX

Most people do not understand the idea of real relaxation. Ask a group of friends how they relax and you'll get as many different answers as there are people in the group. Many times we are fooled into thinking we are relaxing, but nothing could be further from the truth. Learn to breathe correctly to really begin the relaxation process. Look at a baby breathe ....notice how the stomach fills up like a balloon and the chest never moves. This is called diaphragmatic breathing. Teach your lover (and yourself) to breathe properly, especially in a tense or stressful situation. Using your diaphragm (a muscle that sits under the rib cage like a platter) is easy if you practice a little. As you inhale, make believe that you are filling up an imaginary balloon in your stomach. If you have some difficulty moving your diaphragm, you can clasp your fingers together and hold your hands behind your neck. You can also lie back in a recliner or on the bed or couch. This will help you move the diaphragm much easier.

Breathe in slowly for a count of five. Hold the breath for a count of five then exhale for a count of seven. You can always exhale longer then you can inhale. Repeat this sequence four or five times and remember .... do it slowly. You actually change the chemical state of your body and you can feel the difference. Relaxing properly also helps you boost your immune system.

When you are stressed, you are unable to rapidly process information in your mind. I'll prove it to you. Have you ever had an argument with someone? Three hours later as you were thinking about it, you began to say, "I should have said this, or I should have said that." Where is all this good stuff coming from now? Where was it when you needed it three hours ago? The stress of the moment prevented you from retrieving it quickly from your mind.

The same thing happens to a child who has test anxiety. The child can study with the parent all week and know all the answers to all the questions on the test backwards! If the child has test anxiety, the moment the teacher drops the booklet on the desk, the child freezes. You get to question number three and you know the answer, you went over it with your parent four times last night but you can't think of it. If you relax (doing the breathing) this will help your ability to recall function much faster.

## More information on relaxation can be found at:

http://www.mindbodygreen.com/0-4386/A-Simple-Breathing-Exercise-to-Calm-Your-Mind-Body.html

www.JimCullumHypnosis.com

http://www.health.harvard.edu/newsletters/Harvard_Womens_Health_Watch/2008/July/relaxation_techniques_breath_focus

Use this space for notes, thoughts and your own ideas:

# RELAX BY MEDITATION

You can buy books, CD's, MP3's and DVD's that have meditation programs on them. Use the WEB sites mentioned above or enter "learn to meditate" in your search engine. Learning to meditate is fun and very relaxing. This is something that can be done alone, for another person or with another person. A good meditation can take from about 15 to 45 minutes. Adjust the temperature of the room you use so you can feel comfortable. If you are wearing any tight or restrictive clothing, loosen it to allow a comfortable circulation in your body. A recliner works great, but a couch, sofa and even a mat on the floor works well. You can allow your partner to experience a relaxation alone or you can do it together. Finding a quiet and comfortable place, whether indoors or out will provide a good starting point for this exercise.

# DINNER CRUISES

If you like to have fun and listen to live music with dinner and dancing, you should consider taking your lover on a dinner cruise. Obviously you'll need to be close enough to "water" for this event, but it is fun and enjoyable. I've been on dinner cruises on both rivers and the ocean. One dinner cruise was informal with a live band and dancing. The food was served buffet style and they had an open bar. The people dressed casually. Another dinner cruise was more formal; jackets and ties were required. The boat was much larger and it was a sit down dinner. There was live music and dancing as well. There was even a theatrical production put on by the waiters and waitresses. Each dinner cruise lasted about three to four hours. You can check your local paper for more information or do a WEB search for "dinner cruise" and then enter your location.

# CRUISES

If you really want to impress your honey take her on a cruise! Cruise ships are huge, just like floating hotels.  When you book a cruise, the only additional money you spend will be for drinks, tips, and things such as gifts, massages, beauty shop, casino gambling, etc. Your food comes with the trip and you can eat all you want on a cruise. The food is literally non-stop and you can eat till you bust. If you enjoy eating, you really should consider taking a cruise.

Rooms on a cruise ship come in many different varieties.  Some are very small and deep inside the ship with no windows. On the other hand, you can have a suite with sliding glass doors onto your own private balcony. The bigger the space you occupy, the more costly your rate.  Smaller rooms have smaller bathrooms with toilet, sink and shower only. Larger rooms or suites provide two vanity sinks with tub and shower. You are basically paying for space on a cruise ship.

There is lots of entertainment on a cruise ship such as live comedians, stage shows and several lounges where you can dance to music or sip your favorite drink with the one you love. There are casinos for gambling and boutique shops that sell just about anything you might be looking for. There are swimming pools, hot tubs and even a jogging track. Some ships have rock climbing walls and much more. Every night there are deck parties or BBQ's and that is in addition to your dinner.

Remember, cruise ships are big, about the size of almost three football fields in length. Modern computer technology helps stabilize the ships for a comfortable voyage through the ocean. It rained one day on a cruise we were on and there was so much to do on this large vessel, we hardly noticed the inclement weather at all.

You can take ocean cruises to just about anywhere in the world. They can last from two nights to several weeks or more. There are also river cruises that explore rivers and towns all around the globe as well.

To learn more about taking a cruise you can check these WEB sites:

http://www.cruisedirectonline.com/whytakeacruise.htmh

http://cruiseknowledge.com

http://woodburytravel.com

# CONCERTS AND PLAYS

Concerts are given all year round and held in many different venues. There are free concerts held in parks and community centers locally as well as top dollar productions held in large stadiums. If your honey likes a particular group, person or style of music, check the internet for possible appearances in your area. Tickets can be bought for a great night out as well as given as a gift.

You don't have to live near Broadway to experience fabulous plays. If your honey has expressed an interest in seeing something being presented at a local venue, take the hint. Quality productions can be seen all over the world. Many Broadway productions "go on the road" and perform in a few different cities before coming back to New York.

You can check your local newspapers or some of the WEB sites I've listed below for concert and theater tickets:

http://www.jambase.com

http://www.stubhub.com/concert-tickets

http://www.ticketmaster.com/about/about-us.html

# SPORTING EVENTS

If your honey is truly a fan of sporting events, by all means keep her happy. Attending games, whether local or away can be a great way to share time together. Attending a local game can be a great way to have a day trip and attending an away game can be a fun way to enjoy a multiple day trip as well.

You can buy your tickets locally if you live near the stadium or you can visit these WEB sites for more information:

https://seatgeek.com

http://www.ticketmaster.com/section/sports

http://www.cheaptickets.com/events/categories/sports-tickets

# RENAISSANCE FAIRS

A fun-filled day can be had by anyone attending a renaissance fair. If you like the Middle Ages, jousting, partying, song and dance, costumes and so much more, you'll enjoy a renaissance fair. They are usually held on weekends and in several different locations around the country.

You can see pirates, glass blowing, archery contests, jugglers and magicians. There are street vendors selling food and jewelry as well as costumes of the period. You can also view short theatrical productions and participate in certain games and contests and so much more.

We once drove out of state to attend a renaissance fair and it rained most of the day but we still had a wonderful time. They sold disposable ponchos for a few dollars to keep you dry as you walked around. There were also several covered areas and many of the attractions were indoors.

For more information about what a renaissance fair is and attending one near you, please visit:

http://www.renfaire.com

http://www.renaissancemagazine.com/fairelist.html

http://www.therenlist.com/fairs

# IMPORTANT INFORMATION YOU MIGHT WANT TO KNOW:

In this section, I provide you with a very valuable reference tool. Fill in as much information as you are able. Married people should be able to do this a bit easier than people in a dating relationship. When it is time to give a gift to your honey, you can refer to the information on the following pages to help you get the best gift for her. By knowing this information, it will make it easier for you to choose the perfect gift for your honey and for the occasion.


Her Birthday:

_____

Anniversary date(s)  (if applicable)

_____

_____

_____

_____

Date you first met:

_____

Dates important to her:

Occasion:                              Date:

_____

_____

_____

Her favorite perfume:

_____

Her favorite flower:

_____

Her favorite color:

_____

Her hair color- (note – this can change)

_____

Her eye color-

_____

Her height:

_____

Her weight:

_____

Note: - All sizes can change over time:

Clothing sizes can also change by manufacturer:

Her dress size:

_____

Her blouse size:

_____

Her pants size:

_____

Her shoe size:

_____

Her ring size:

_____

Her favorite food(s):

_____

_____

Her favorite drink:

_____

Her favorite dessert:

_____

Her favorite restaurant:

_____

Her favorite music:

_____

Her favorite movies:

_____

Her favorite books:

_____

_____

_____

Does she have any allergies:

(foods, flowers, materials, etc.)

_____

_____

_____

Is there anything she absolutely dislikes (so you can avoid it):

_____

_____

_____

_____

_____

_____

_____

_____

Let us always meet eachother with a smile, for the smile is the beginning of love.

- Mother Teresa

Use this space for notes, thoughts and your own ideas:

# A THOUGHT TO END ON:

Please note, I am NOT a therapist, not a psychologist nor a councilor. I do not do therapy or treatment of any kind. I have expressed many ideas in this book that have worked well for me and seem to have impressed many others. Ninety-nine percent of what I am sharing with you is just common sense as far as I am concerned. If you read the "Good Book" it states to "Do unto others ......" From another point of view, simply treat others as you desire to be treated.

One more note to consider. An important fact to remember is this: Just because you like someone, care about someone, love someone, or do the wonderful things mentioned in this book for someone, there is no guarantee that they will like you or love you back. Neither kindness nor money can make anyone love you. They have to want to do that on their own. By applying the different possibilities I have outlined in this book, others will see you as a wonderful person worthy of sharing a relationship.

# ABOUT THE AUTHOR

Jim Cullum is a consultant-in-hypnosis, instructor of stress management and relaxation training and personal coach with over 40 years of experience helping people discover their unlimited potential. He gives lectures and workshops around the country. He produced and hosted the live, weekly radio program, "Body, Mind & Spirit Connection," where he interviewed guests on health, healing and wellness.

Jim has always been involved in working with or helping others. He was a volunteer firefighter for over twenty years. He has been an instructor in the cardiac rehab program of a major teaching hospital for twenty years. He is on the board of directors of Irving House, a not-for-profit 501 (c)(3) corporation that fosters animals with special needs.

Jim enjoys several hobbies such as kayaking, fencing, hot air balloons and working with stained glass. When he wants to get away, he likes to relax on a cruise ship and explore all the sights along the way. He also enjoys finding new ways to surprise the people in his life that he cares about.

If you enjoyed reading this book, please consider posting a review on:

www.Amazon.com


Thank you and the best of everything to you and your honey!


Jim

Made in the USA
Charleston, SC
22 January 2015